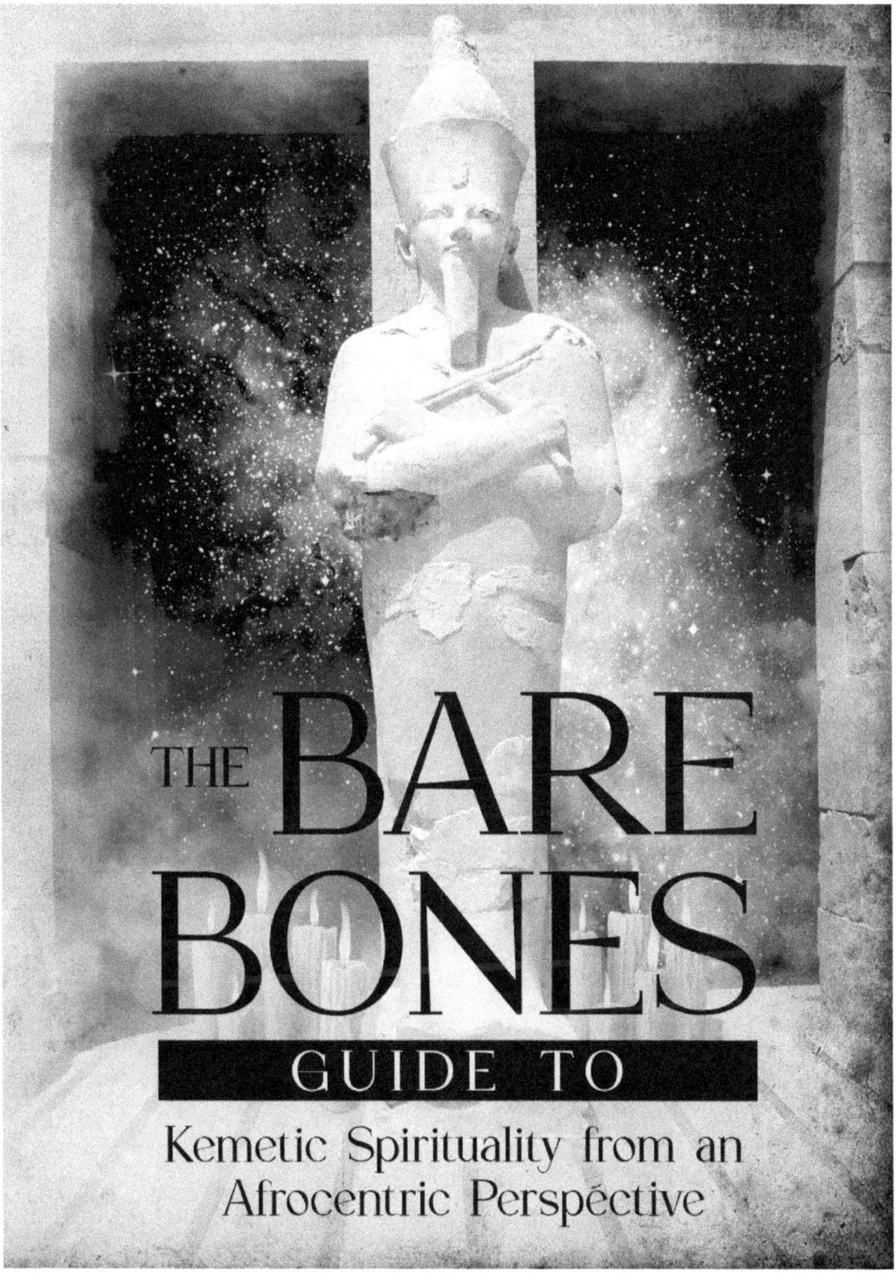

THE BARE BONES
BONES
GUIDE TO
Kemetic Spirituality from an
Afrocentric Perspective

COPYRIGHT © 2024 Derric Moore

All rights reserved. No part of this publication may be reproduced or transmitted in any form or by any means, electronic or mechanical, including photocopying, recording or by any information storage and retrieval system, without written permission from the author, except for the inclusion of brief quotation in a review. The information contained in this book is intended to be educational and not for diagnosis, prescription, or treatment of any health disorder whatsoever. This information should not replace consultation with a competent healthcare professional. The content of the book is intended to be used as an adjunct to a rational and responsible healthcare program prescribed by a licensed healthcare practitioner. This is a book about faith. As such the author and publisher do not warrant the success any person would have used any of the exercises and techniques contained herein. Success and failure will vary. The author and publisher therefore are in no way liable for any misuse of the material contained herein.

Historical images and figurines public domain courtesy of Wikimedia Commons

Illustrations courtesy of Jeff Dahl, CC BY-SA 4.0, via Wikimedia Commons

Illustrations courtesy of Dreamstine.com

Additional Illustrations courtesy of Pexels.com

WARNING & DISCLAIMER

Every effort has been made to make this book as accurate and as complete as possible. However, there may be both content and typographical errors within. Therefore, this text should be used as a general guide. Please consider all the information within this book is intended to be educational and entertainment, and not for speculation, not for accounting, not for legal, and not for medical advice or professional advice. This information should not replace consultation with a competent healthcare professional. This information should not replace consultation with a competent healthcare professional. The content of the book is intended to be used as an adjunct to a rational and responsible healthcare program prescribed by a licensed healthcare professional. Therefore, the information within should be used at your own risk. You, the reader needs to do your own due diligence to determine if the content within this book is right for you.

Although, every attempt has been made to verify the information within this book. Neither the author, publisher or affiliates shall have liability or responsibility to any person, group, or entity with respect to any damage or loss caused or alleged to be caused directly or indirectly by the information within this book. Neither the author, publisher or affiliates shall have liability or responsibility for contrary interpretation of the subject matter, errors, or omissions. The information within this book is provided on the understanding that you, the reader, will use it in accordance with the laws of your country.

For individuals who love to find mistakes, please send your corrections to the author for the next edition.

To protect the identity and privacy of others, all the names within this book have been adapted, modified, and changed for confidentiality purposes. Any alleged slights to any specific person(s), or organization(s) are purely unintentional.

eBook: ISBN: 979-8-9865739-1-5

Print: ISBN: 979-8-9865739-2-2

TABLE OF CONTENTS

ACKNOWLEDGMENTS VI
AUTHOR'S PREFACE VIII
CHAPTER 1 INTRODUCTION 1
    CHAPTER 2: FIRST THINGS FIRST. WHAT IS KEMETIC SPIRITUALITY? 5
CHAPTER 3: THE TRUTH ABOUT SPIRIT GUIDES 18
  CHAPTER 4: WHAT ARE THE ANCESTORS AND WHY SHOULD WE HONOR THEM? 24
   CHAPTER 5: HOW TO BUILD AN ALTAR FOR YOUR AAKHU (ANCESTORS & SPIRIT GUIDES) 32
CHAPTER 6: WHAT ARE THE NETCHARU (GUARDIAN SPIRITS) AND HOW DO YOU BUILD AN ALTAR FOR THEM? 42
   CHAPTER 7: HOW TO HONOR & PETITION THE NETCHARU (GUARDIAN SPIRITS) 69
CONCLUSION 73

ACKNOWLEDGMENTS

Thank you, Nebertchar, God, Lord of All, and Supreme Being of All. You are all I know, and everything I don't understand. Thank you for creating the beautiful and sacred Universe surrounding me and the lovely and holy Universe within me.

Thank you, Netcharu, magnificent guardian spirits who defend God's mysteries. Thank you for encouraging me and highlighting the value of communal energy in effecting change. Thank you for your legends, stories, folklore, myths, and mystical manifestations. These have helped me recognize that leaders are fantastic focal points for group aims. Still, some things don't require a leader. Some things we can achieve for ourselves simply by collaborating with others who share our values. We can improve the quality of life for all by collaborating and working together.

Thank you, Aakhu, for accepting my petition for cultural change and supporting me in bringing about healing. Thanks also to those long and forgotten whose blood flows through me and who have called me to tell their stories.

Thanks to my family and friends for your love and support and for agreeing to disagree until further notice.

Thanks to my wife, daughter, and in-laws, who have taught me about myself as I have learned more about you.

This book is a thank you to everyone who assisted me and a tribute to our forefathers' wisdom. It was designed to 1) remind us of our sacred obligation and 2) inspire us to do better. 2) For our "family" so that when they become conscious of themselves. This book can be used as a reference guide to assist them in developing a stronger relationship with our Ancestors and Spirit Guides. Thank you once more for your encouragement, support, and criticism.

AUTHOR'S PREFACE

"If everything of substance was taken from a slave (reading, culture, language, etc.), why was Christianity allowed?"
- David Banner.

We are all God's Children, but Africans did not need anyone to tell them this because, contrary to popular belief, people of African descent did not have or practice a religion per se. We practiced spiritual systems, which inspired us to become "Men and Women of God." What's the difference between religion and spiritual systems, you ask?

Originating in Latin, the word "religion" is thought to have come from the verb "religare," which means "to bind" or "to connect." This means that religion forces people to adhere to beliefs, doctrines, customs, or ideas about a supreme being. In other words, religion is a set of dos and don'ts, which historically were created by the dominant individuals of society on how all citizens are expected to act and behave. Hence, most religions are artificial. On the other hand, spiritual systems are a set of organic practices based upon cultural beliefs and principles that promote better health, physical and mental advancement, and overall well-being for the individual and the community.

Hence, spiritual systems are community and nature based. If you were to study African history, you would learn that Africa's Golden Age was when Kush (ancient Nubia) and later Kemet (ancient Egypt) were the world's innovators. Besides building the pyramids, both ancient African societies had mastered mathematics, the arts, and sciences, which allowed their society to exist for hundreds and thousands of years. However, after the rise and spread of Christianity and Islam throughout the African continent, black people began to regress. They ceased being inventors and originators for their benefit. In other words, everything that black people produced became the sole property of foreigners.

An analysis of history will reveal that religion has never served our best interest. Religion has always retarded our spiritual growth, divided our community, and benefited those who are alien to our culture. Throughout the Afro-Diaspora, our communities are devastated by poverty. At the same time, religious institutions such as mega-churches thrive and continue to amass more significant amounts of wealth. The only way for us to return our greatness is by abandoning man-made religions that have never served us or our community and reclaiming our ancestral spiritual systems that have, since time immemorial, advanced us.

Hetepu (Peace & Blessings)
December 21, 2023
Derric Moore

CHAPTER 1
Introduction

This small book aims to provide insight into practicing this tradition to those interested in Kemetic spirituality from an Afrocentric perspective. I initially wrote this little book to quickly answer questions that my nephews and nieces asked me when they entered my home and saw my Ancestor's altar. So, this book will not delve deeply into the philosophy behind my practice. As the title indicates, it is a *Bare Bares Guide to Kemetic Spirituality from an Afrocentric Perspective*.

I always tell people a little bit about myself so that people will understand that practicing Kemetic spirituality has nothing to do with your background or religious affiliation. Also, Kemetic spirituality is not anti-religion, anti-God, or anti-Christian. Kemetic spirituality is commonly compared and contrasted with Christianity so that people can see the differences between the two. This is important to understand because it is commonly believed that if you are not Christian, you don't believe in God. Quite the contrary, I believe wholeheartedly in, or rather, I know, God, but I also believe in mathematics and science.

You see, unlike Western religions, where God and science are separated and at odds with each other, God is used as a safety point to refer back to when things go awry. Kemetic spirituality teaches that we are Children of God who will one day become men and women of God, hence a god and goddess. The difference between a Child of God and a Man and Woman of God will be explained in *Chapter 3: What are Ancestors and Why Should We Honor Them?* This unique approach to the Supreme Being establishes God as humanity's first, most significant, and oldest Ancestor. Therefore, we all pay homage to God in everything that we do.

Science is a systematic endeavor that constructs and arranges knowledge through universe-related hypotheses and testable explanations. Science is used to confirm our godliness. For instance, in Western religions, we are taught that if we want positive change, we should have faith and pray for a miracle in hopes that God favors and blesses us. From a Kemetic spirituality perspective, this approach to God is too vague, has too many ambiguities, and creates the notion that God plays favorites. Therefore, if God favors us, we are blessed, but if we are not favored, we are not blessed, which makes us not receiving a blessing God's fault.

For this reason, in Kemetic spirituality, we are taught that God is a Benevolent and Perfect Being whose blessings are like the rays of the Sun, which means that when we do not receive a blessing. The fault lies on us (humanity), which means we are doing something that causes misalignment or blocks God's blessings (rays of the Sun). Therefore, if we want positive change, we are told to pray or meditate to God for positive change, but in addition. We are also given a specific prescription on what behaviors we must adopt and cultivate or our current actions and behaviors obstructing us from receiving God's blessings (rays).

This unique understanding is why most people practicing Kemetic spirituality feel as if they are called to do so and typically have some story that conveys their beliefs. My story is that I am a preacher kid who grew up in a very devout Christian household. As a child, I loved the singing and even the fiery sermons of the preacher, but when I got older, I noticed no spiritual growth.

The preacher was preaching the same message with a different title because I learned later that they didn't understand the metaphysics of the human soul. This realization inspired me to leave the Church, and in the process, I met my first spirit guide. For the next ten years or so, I read and studied Kemetic history, African history, metaphysics, psychology, folklore, mysticism, and the occult until I met my mentor Papa, an Afro-Cuban priest in the Lucumi (Santeria) religion and practicing Spiritist, who taught me the spiritual traditions that could not be found in a book. Then, some time afterward, I became deathly ill and was diagnosed with systemic lupus. To heal my body and recover from the illness, I turned to everything I had learned about the Kemetic traditions combined with what Papa had taught me.

For the record, so that there is no confusion or misunderstanding, I am not telling you that Kemetic spirituality cured me or gave me a miracle cure. What I am telling you is that 16 years later, the illness has gone into remission. I am healthy because I combined my understanding of the Kemetic tradition with the teachings of Papa, which resulted in what could best be called Afro-Kemetic spirituality. Through Afro-Kemetic spirituality, I learned how to tap into the Divine power within me and how to use that power to heal myself.

There are many Afro-Kemetic spiritual paths where African descendants syncretize Kemetic philosophy and theology with contemporary African or Afro-Diasporic religions and traditions. The path you are about to read about in this little book is the Afro-Kemetic path that I call Kamta. It draws its inspiration from Kemetic theology, Bantu-Kongo philosophy, African American folk beliefs and practices, and Espiritismo Cruzado (Afro-Cuban Crossed Spiritism).

Through this book, I aim to answer the most frequently asked questions about Kemetic and Afro-Kemetic spirituality and explain how to get started. I will not go into detail about the different

Kemetic paths because it would take us beyond the scope of this book. Instead, I hope this book will be used as a reference guide to assist you in your progress.

CHAPTER 2:
First Things First.
What Is Kemetic Spirituality?

The towering temples, colossal pyramids, and elaborate hieroglyphics of the ancient Egyptians, also known as the Kemetic civilization, are testaments to people with an intimate connection with the divine. The mysteries of the Kemetic spiritual heritage, which have inspired wonder and captivated human imagination for millennia, are at the core of this society. The Kemetic spiritual traditions have been revived and adapted. They are referred to today as Kemetic spirituality due to the appeal of the Kemetic spiritual heritage that transcends religious devotion and cultural and geographic barriers.

So, what is Kemetic spirituality?

Kemetic spirituality is a contemporary movement that draws inspiration from ancient Egypt's religious, cultural, and philosophical traditions. There are five critical elements of contemporary Kemetic spirituality, and they are:

- The movement's primary source of inspiration comes from the pantheon, spiritual rituals, and respect for nature found in the Kemetic philosophical traditions.
- Adherence to the Principles of Ma'a(t) embodies truth, justice, harmony, and balance. Consequently, practitioners

of Kemetic spirituality strive to align their lives with these principles, seeking balance and righteousness in their actions.
- The veneration of the Ancestors is where practitioners honor their ancestors to obtain guidance and wisdom from them.
- Fostering and nurturing a deep connection to nature by revering and celebrating nature, such as performing rituals that mark the cycles of the season, like winter and summer solstice, equinoxes, etc., and finally.
- The process by which practitioners adapt and syncretize traditions, adding features and current insights to make Kemetic spirituality more relevant in the present era.

What is Afro-Kemetic Spirituality?

Kemetic spirituality has grown in popularity among African descendants as a means of examining and commemorating African spirituality apart from the effects of colonization and the transatlantic slave trade.

For descendants of Africa, particularly those living in the Americas, Kemetic spirituality is a means of reclaiming their cultural heritage. It provides a chance to investigate African religious customs before colonization and establish a bond with a legacy shattered by the Transatlantic Slave Trade. For this reason, Kemetic spirituality offers African descendants a framework for cultural pride, self-discovery, and a sense of connection to a larger African spiritual history, thereby empowering and defining their identity. This realization led to the creation of the phrase "Afro-Kemetic spirituality."

What's the Difference Between the Two?

The distinct difference between Kemetic and Afro-Kemetic spirituality is that Kemetic spirituality practitioners typically draw inspiration from Western traditions such as Wicca and other New Age practices. Many Kemetic spirituality practitioners generally use the Greco-Roman names of the Kemetic deities like Osiris, Isis, Anubis, Thoth, etc. Also, most Kemetic spirituality practitioners rely heavily on archeologists' and historians' interpretations of the Kemetic tradition. As a result, most Kemetic spirituality practitioners can be classified as either Kemetic Reconstructionist who seek to reestablish or reconstruct the Kemetic religion with as much scholarly knowledge and comparative religion as possible or as Kemetic Wiccans - practitioners blend Kemetic deities with contemporary Wiccan practices and rites.

But in Afro-Kemetic spirituality, since African religions and traditions have been severely disrupted because of colonization and the transatlantic slave trade, historically, Western scholars have demonized non-Western faiths and traditions, such as Vodun, Santeria, Hoodoo, etc., and non-Western traditions to support racist institutions throughout the Western world. In Afro-Kemetic spirituality, there is a strong focus on Kemetic history and Kemet's correlation to Sub-Saharan African history or Afrocentricity, which is often separated and classified as Middle Eastern history despite Kemet being on the African continent.

I will not entertain the debate on if the Kemetic people were Black or non-Black here because there's countless amount of archeological, historical, linguistic, and DNA evidence that reveals even if all the Kemetic people did not have the "classical Negroid features" of dark skin, broad nose, and curly hair as the first Greek historian Herodotus described. Generally speaking, the Kemetic people, from a cultural perspective, were a Black civilization before being invaded by the Hyksos, the Persians, the Greeks, the Romans, and finally, the Islamic, Ottoman, and Arab conquests, which currently dominates the entire North, East, and West of the Africa continent.

Acknowledging that the Kemet was a Black African civilization means that Kemet had similar spiritual beliefs and practices as other traditional Africans, as noted by numerous scholars, including Sir E. A. Wallis Budge in his book *Osiris and the Egyptian Resurrection,* such as the Akan, Ewe, Yoruba, Kongo, and other African ethnic groups.

Consequently, traditional African philosophy is the primary source for reestablishing and reconstructing the Kemetic tradition. Archeologists' and historians' interpretations of the Kemetic tradition are used only as a last resort.

Is Kemetic Spirituality Monotheistic or Polytheistic?

Although some may argue that race and ethnicity should not matter; the reason Afro-Kemetic spirituality practitioners emphasize race is because of the noted cultural difference between Black Africans and non-Africans. For instance, in the 19th and early 20th centuries, archeologists and historians reported that the Kemetic people had a polytheistic belief system, meaning they worshipped idols. A closer look at the Kemetic spiritual practices and the surviving texts, such as the *Pert em Hru* (incorrectly called the *Egyptian Book of the Dead*), indicates that Kemetic people were not polytheistic in the true sense of the word because the Kemetic people had always believed that there was only one Supreme Being (even before the birth of Akhenaten) whom they called Nebertchar – The Lord of All Things. However, the Kemetic were not strictly monotheistic because they understood that the Nebertchar could manifest itself in numerous forms.

Attempting to classify the Kemetic people as being monotheistic or polytheistic has always been challenging because, according to many Afro-Kemetic spiritual practitioners, the Kemetic people did not have a religion in the classical sense. Religion is a codified system of worship or dogma centering around a specific deity or deity that occurs in a particular place. But when we look at the divinities in the Kemetic tradition, we will not find a system of codes, dogma, etc., because the Kemetic people practiced a syncretic system of religions.

For instance, one of the most popular divinities in the Kemetic tradition is the dog, jackal, or wolf-headed (masked) netchar Anubis, Enpu, or Npu (shown above), who is recognized as the guide of the dead. Still, no records suggest that Npu was worshipped all over ancient Kemet. Npu only appeared and took an active role in the Kemetic tradition when guiding souls in the afterlife. Another example of this can be seen in the fact that the ibis-headed Thoth, Djehuty, or Djahuti was not worshipped all over Kemet but only appeared in Kemetic lore to fulfill his role, which was to resolve conflict through "magical" means. The same can be said about all the netcharu, which only appear to perform a specific role.

From an Afro-Kemetic perspective, Kemetic spirituality is neither monotheistic nor polytheistic, which acknowledges a single deity that takes preeminence over all the other deities. Kemetic spirituality is based upon the belief in ONE GOD and a host of divinities called in the Kemetic language Netchar and the netcharu (or part netcharu), like the Yoruba Olodumare and the orishas, the Kongo Nzambi and nkisi, Nyame and the abosom, and many other traditional African religions and traditions.

This understanding is what has led many to believe that Kemetic Spirituality is like many traditional African religions that blend monotheistic and polytheistic elements. The inability to see Kemetic Spirituality as an ancient African Spiritual system is due to the refusal to acknowledge that Kemet is a Black and brown-skinned African civilization. Thus, labeling Kemetic Spirituality as a polytheistic belief system is done by individuals who either are too impatient and lazy to develop a proper understanding of the Kemetic philosophy and are following an agenda to discredit, disorganize, and demonize the Kemetic people and their descendants (Africans who spiritual systems descend from same Nilotic root) by referring to their belief system as polytheistic.

Then, What are the Netcharu are they Gods and Goddesses?

When it is accepted that the Kemetic people were Black Africans and that their Spirituality is like other traditional Africans. We find that the Kemetic people believed in one omnipotent, omniscient, omnipresent, and distant GOD, who does not directly interact with humanity and takes on different names such as Netchar (Neter, Netjer, pronounced as Nature), Nebertcher (the Lord of All Things, hence the Source), Amun Ra (the Hidden Creator), and so on. The one GOD - Netchar is described as a distant Creator to indicate that the essence of GOD lies within.

Ra is not the sun god or the sun, which is called "aten" in the Kemetic language. Ra is a solar force (the life force or the power of GOD) that Netchar created to make life possible throughout the universe. Through the Ra (the life force, solar force, or power of God), the masculine Shu and feminine Tefnut were created, followed by the ethereal mother Nyut (Nut) and the physical father, Geb. Through these influences, the netcharu (divinities) were created.

Kemetic lore states that the netcharu walked the earth to make life habitable. To ensure that people can connect to Netchar, the netcharu acts as an emissary to Netchar and a divine guide and guardian for humanity. When the netcharu ascended back into the heavens, humans referred to the life of the netcharu as a guide. Therefore, from an Afro-Kemetic perspective, Netchar created everything in the universe and, finally, humanity so that it could experience life. In other words, Netchar made the netcharu as signposts to help It return to Its original state of being.

Therefore, the netcharu (sometimes spelled neteru or netjeru), derived from the Kemetic term Netchar (Nature), are the most celebrated and recognized characters within the Kemetic tradition because they are not gods and goddesses but are archetypes, aspects, attributes, and principles of Nature or Netchar. In other words, the netcharu are what physicists call today atomic structures, which the Kemetic people personified.

Why Were the Netcharu Personified?

It is simple: how else would you explain to farmers and other laypeople so that they can improve the quality of their lives that our universe is composed of energy and that there are positive and negative forces, with a positive and negative charge called a proton, electrons, and a central force called a neutron?

Answer: You would begin by saying the central force Ra created the proton Shu and the electron Tefnut, etc. Now, when it is stated that the netcharu or the gods and goddesses walked the earth, understand the authors are referring to energy or forces of Netchar (Nature), not actual physical mystical beings. For the record, the same can be said about other supernatural beings, such as giants.

As you can see, the Kemetic spiritual systems are thousands of years older than Judaism, Christianity, and Islam. It should be clear that the archeologists and historians who interpreted the Kemetic spiritual texts either were ignorant of physics and other sciences or deliberately chose to report the Kemetic peoples' scientific reasoning to promote the idea that Westerners are superior, and that Judeo-Christianity is the only and true monotheistic religion of the world.

Unfortunately, because Western scholars have interpreted the Kemetic spiritual texts literally, many people are confused and under the impression surreal mystical creatures are floating around in our universe waiting for sacrifices. Once it is understood that the netcharu are the personification of the forces of Netchar (Nature) that exist outside and within us (since we are also a product of the universe).

It also becomes clear that there is no right or wrong way to interpret or interact with the netcharu because they are atoms, electrons, protons, leptons, neutrinos, and quarks that exist within and outside us. Therefore, it is our actions and behaviors that created the netcharu. We are the creators of the netcharu. Specifically, every word we utter, every gesture we make, every action, behavior, etc., creates the positive and negative forces or netcharu that exist in our life, which the Kemetic people call specific names. For instance, if you are hateful and selfish to others, you cause the chaotic netchar Set to come into your life. On the other hand, if you are peaceful and selfless, you generate another nectar like Osar to enter your life.

This means that you can shake your fist at God all you want when tragedy hits. You can fuss and ask why God has cursed you when things go wrong, but the reality is that we are the cause of our blessings and curses. Once the nature of the netcharu is truly understood, it becomes clear that the netcharu exists because they help us become the creators of our realities and the masters of destinies. In other words, the netcharu make us responsible for our actions and behaviors and are, thus, guardian spirits.

According to Kemetic lore, there are ten guardian spirits or permanent netcharu whom I'll introduce to you soon. However, before doing so, we must fully comprehend who the netcharu are as guardian spirits. We must first understand the Kemetic ethics and philosophies or the Maa that caused them to exist.

Understanding the Principles of Maa(t)

According to the oldest religious text in the world, the Kemetic text *The Book of Knowing the Manifestations of Ra and Overthrowing Apep (also called The Book of Knowing the Transformations of Ra and Overthrowing Apep),* after the Divine as Nebertchar created Itself. Its first act of creation was to establish balance, order, and reciprocity, which it accomplished by creating an ancient primeval mound that emerged out of chaos called Maa, symbolizing a stable foundation that creation could be built upon.

It is essential to understand that Maa is not a concept that the Kemetic people created. The Maa is a true force of nature that the Kemetic sages discovered, which could be measured and quantified like a science. As a result, the term Maa, which means order, balance, harmony, justice, and truth, is commonly symbolized as the Feather of Truth. This means Maa (order, balance, harmony, justice, and truth) is not subjective or based on our biases, emotions, personal beliefs, and prejudices.

Therefore, Maa is the foundational principle governing physical and spiritual realms. It signifies the cosmic order that ensures the proper working of the seasons' cycles and the importance of justice, ethical behavior, and morality within a community.

Nothing is above Maa. Everything, including Netchar itself, adhered to the principles of Maa. To indicate and remind people who adhered to the principles of Maa that they would be protected and blessed in the physical and spiritual realm. Maa was personified as the netchart Ma'at (Maat), frequently depicted as a woman with outstretched arms as wings, wearing a single ostrich feather headdress symbolizing truth and righteousness. Due to Christian ethics and morality views, many believe that being honest and performing acts of kindness are the only expressions of Maa, but this is only the tip of the ancient primeval mound (pun intended). When it is kept in mind that Maa ensures that everything that comes into existence is orderly, balanced, and in harmony, thus making everything just and establishing truth.

It becomes evident that the Kemetic people held a high regard for Maa because Maa gave purpose to everything that existed, which means that everything that exists, whether known or not, has a purpose or Divine Purpose for existing.

This means that synchronicities are always present, and if we develop our psychic senses, we can perceive the spiritual reality and detect the omens and signs that will reveal the Maa. Synchronicities can be considered "being at the right place at the right time." Therefore, the next time something falls like food on the floor or an event occurs unexpectedly, such as you are delayed and running late for work. It is easy to get upset and see this as a problem, but if you remember that because of the Maa, everything is connected and working together harmoniously by attempting to know the significance of such occurrences from a positive perspective. It is possible to see the Maa. For instance, the food falling could be interpreted as a sign that a hungry spirit is near. Being delayed by a traffic jam could prevent you from having a severe accident, and so on.

Since the spiritual realm, unlike the physical realm, is vast and diverse, there are unlimited reasons why synchronistic events occur. So many Kemetic practitioners use a divination tool or oracle to help them see the Maa (the truth or the whole spiritual and physical reality), which some refer to as interpreting the will of Netchar. This is based upon the belief and understanding that the Divine knows everything and has orchestrated everything flawlessly.

From this understanding, our Universe is Perfect because Netchar is Perfect, and everything it created is Perfect. Practically speaking, this means that there are no such things as accidents or coincidences because Maa ensures that divine machinations and calculations are always at work. Because of the Maa, the Divine ensures that the helpful stranger who happens to show up is at the right place and when we need them.

We think accidents, coincidences, or events suddenly occur because we do not normally perceive our universe's hidden, invisible spiritual reality. Most of us only focus on the physical reality.

This understanding forces us to ask: If our universe is perfect because it was created by a Netchar, who is a Perfect Being, then why does evil exist in our world, or more importantly?

Why does Netchar allow evil to exist?

The short answer is that evil exists because of isfet (chaos, disorder, and imbalance). The long answer is that we do not see the whole picture, and as a result, we don't realize we are all connected through the Divine. Evil exists because humanity makes choices and decisions that conflict with the Maa (the Divine Order). Therefore, to avoid bringing evil into the world, the solution is to connect with the Spirits (ancestors, spirit guides, guardian spirits, etc.).

Honoring the ancestors and venerating the spirit guides is appropriate because the ancestors and spirit guides are familiar with the physical realm but reside in the spiritual realm. It is believed that the ancestors can see both physical and spiritual realities and thus offer guidance and wisdom to help the living navigate the sea of life.

CHAPTER 3:
The Truth About Spirit Guides

As I mentioned in chapter one of this book that I met my first spirit guide when I lost my faith in God. Since I was raised in an Apostolic Pentecostal Christian household, I, like many people, did not know anything about angels, spirits, guardian spirits, spirit guides, etc. Because I was required to attend church for so long, I don't remember any bible classes, Sunday school lessons, church summer camps, etc., that explained what spirit guides were and were not, so I had to learn through trial and error.

When I first met my spirit guide, I was very depressed because the media had painted a picture that I, a young black male, would not make it to the age of 18. According to "statistics," I would either be imprisoned or killed by some senseless act of drug-related violence. To escape this onslaught, I tried to be "saved" or receive the "gift of the Holy Ghost," but I failed to keep the Holy Ghost. I don't know why. I could not keep the Holy Ghost and live a godly life, so I concluded that I was not one of the chosen ones (the 144,000) God wanted to save. This meant on top of me having a miserable life where I would end up dead, I was going to go to hell and burn in a lake of fire. So, yeah, I was depressed, but I was also angry as hell at God.

In fact, I was so angry that I gave God the middle finger in hopes of being struck down by lightning so that I could tell God how stupid it was to create me but not allow me to be saved. I wanted to die, and I started doing a lot of things that were considered blasphemous, like questioning everything that I was taught. One of the things I pondered was how the Egyptians accomplished so much, according to the National Geographic magazines I had. Still, the Egyptians were supposed to be evil because they believed in many gods. Yet, Joseph the Dreamer served as an Egyptian pharaoh, and Joseph and Mary fled to Egypt with baby Jesus to escape King Herod. It didn't make sense.

Another thing that didn't make sense was why Moses didn't give the Egyptians the Ten Commandments. It was all too much, and none of the church people I knew could give me a satisfying answer to any of these questions. It all just made me even angrier at God. Eventually, I began contemplating suicide so that I could cuss God out, and that's when I met my spirit guide.

Like many people who have encountered their spirit guides, when I met my spirit guide, I thought I was crazy. I thought I was talking to myself, but my spirit guide confirmed it was real. I wasn't sure if it was real, so I asked it a question. I asked the spirit guide how the Egyptians could have accomplished so much yet be considered evil because they worshipped different gods. The spirit guide answered, or rather, the answer just popped into my head that the Egyptians were not evil and had always known that there was one God. It was weird because it was like I suddenly knew the answer, and the funny thing was that it made all my worries disappear. However, I wasn't 100% convinced, so I asked why Moses didn't give the Ten Commandments to the Egyptians, and instantly, the answer came as soon as I finished thinking about the question. "They didn't need it. The Children of Israel were the ones who were lost."

I was shocked by the quickness of the response but also relieved because it brought profound peace to my young mind. Then, this spirit guide, whom I called the Voice, told me I had so many problems receiving the Holy Ghost because this was not my path. The Voice told me to study the Egyptian religion, and everything would make sense, and that's what I did.

Not long after, everything that the Voice had told me was confirmed. The most significant "a-ha" moment that I had after talking with the Voice was discovering the *42 Declarations or Laws of Maa(t)*:

1- I have not committed sin
2- I have not committed robbery with violence
3- I have not stolen
4- I have not slain men and women
5- I have not stolen food
6- I have not swindled offerings
7- I have not stolen from God
8- I have not told lies
9- I have not carried away food
10- I have not cursed
11- I have not closed my ears to truth
12- I have not committed adultery
13- I have not made anyone cry
14- I have not felt sorrow without reason
15- I have not assaulted anyone
16- I am not deceitful
17- I have not stolen anyone's land
18- I have not been an eavesdropper
19- I have not falsely accused anyone
20- I have not been angry without reason
21- I have not seduced anyone's wife
22- I have not polluted myself
23- I have not terrorized anyone
24- I have not disobeyed the law
25- I have not been excessively angry
26- I have not cursed God
27- I have not behaved with violence
28- I have not caused disruption of peace

29- I have not acted hastily or without thought
30- I have not overstepped my boundaries of concern
31- I have not exaggerated my words when speaking
32- I have not worked evil
33- I have not used evil thoughts, words or deeds
34- I have not polluted the water
35- I have not spoken angrily or arrogantly
36- I have not cursed anyone in thought, word or deed
37- I have not placed myself on a pedestal
38- I have not stolen that which belongs to God
39- I have not stolen from or disrespected the deceased
40- I have not taken food from a child
41- I have not acted with insolence
42- I have not destroyed property belonging to God

I always refer to my experience with the Voice because it led me to this path. Still, I only tried to understand who the Voice was some years later, even though I had a spiritual encounter. I still didn't believe that spirits existed. I knew that spirit guides existed in my soul, but I could not figure it out intellectually. It wasn't until my body became ill and, as I mentioned, I had to take the lessons I had learned from Papa, combined with what I had known about the Egyptian or Kemetic religion, and apply them that my perspective changed.

Consequently, because the Kemetic people had at least five schools of thought or five philosophies on practicing Kemetic spirituality (the Cosmology of Annu, the Cosmology of Khmun, the Cosmology of Thebes, the Cosmology of Men Nefer, and the Cosmology of Aten), in its thousand-year existence, and there were no texts that have been recovered which explain in detail how to practice these philosophies. Numerous theories have risen as to how to practice Kemetic spirituality. The most popular theory is that the Kemetic peoples' spirituality was based on the Tree of Life, which is a map that compares the universe with the human mind. This means that the deities in the Kemetic pantheon are not gods and goddesses but symbols representing different levels of consciousness. Attached to these other levels are our spirit guides.

That being said, all spirit guides are projections of ourselves, thus a part of our Higher Self. They may be the memory of a deceased loved one or someone who never physically existed. Whatever the case, they are archetypes of the whole that help us to find ourselves. Thus, spirit guides are real. We all have at least one spirit guide that can communicate to us in our dreams or intuitively, such as clairaudiently, clairsentiently, clairvoyantly, or claircognizantly. Hence, when something is not right, we may get a feeling, see something out the corner of the eye, hear a strange sound, or get a knowing. We may not be able to explain it logically, but these are all ways our spirit guides communicate to us.

Understanding that our spirit guides are a part of our Higher Self means that our spirit guides are always with us, have always been with us, and will continue to be with us even, regardless of whether we acknowledge their presence. This means we can always communicate with them by asking them for their guidance and insight since they are a part of our Higher Self. Our spirit guides can be whatever we want them to be. Still, they will appear in the most accessible form for us to accept, which means that if you believe they are angels, they will appear as angels. If you think they are gods and goddesses, they will appear as gods or goddesses.

This is important to understand because Western culture, science, and religion have demonized spirituality and made the world fear everything that is not Christian. Consequently, Christians will tell you that spirit guides are masquerading, familiar, trickster, and demonic spirits that will not announce their evil nature but portray themselves as benevolent beings. Many Christians will quote all sorts of biblical scriptures to verify their beliefs but have no problem accepting that an angel (spirit guide) appeared to a virgin woman and told her that she was pregnant. It should be noted that there are numerous biblical examples of angels (spirit guides) interceding on behalf of many biblical heroes and heroines, which Christians cannot replicate.

Here lies the ingenuity of Kemetic sages who mapped the mind thousands of years before the Swiss psychiatrist Carl Jung was born and conceived the idea of the collective unconscious. Thus, they eliminated the guesswork of spiritual development and made spirituality a science.

Communicating with the spirit guides and making offerings is an elaborate way to engage with the Higher Self. Spirit guides will never abandon you or lead you astray. Spirit guides never speak ill of someone or instruct you to do ill to another. Our spirit guides are here to help us fulfill our destiny, and that's their purpose. In the following chapters, you will understand why the Kemetic sages codified our spirit guides.

CHAPTER 4:
What are the Ancestors and Why Should We Honor Them?

Generally speaking, "ancestors" refer to individuals who came before an individual through time and who share a biological connection with them through family ancestry, thus making these individuals older and wiser than us. Therefore, parents, grandparents, great-grandparents, and so on can all be considered ancestors because they guide us in life and inspire us to reach our most significant potential in death. From this understanding, since we all come from the One God, the Creator or Lord of Everything, God is the first ancestor in Afro-Kemetic belief. However, not every ancestor has our best interest at heart. Some ancestors, like people, are confused, misinformed, and just downright evil, which brings me to a significant story and the reason for learning and honoring the ancestors.

When I was a teenager, I struggled with my faith in God. I hung around with three guys at the church because their fathers were also ministers like mine. The oldest of the three guys was this guy whom I will call Jay for disclaimer reasons. I hung around these guys for three reasons.

First, these guys, like me as a teenager, did not like attending church. Second, since Jay was our eldest, he had his driver's license and could trick his parents into letting him keep the car keys. As a result, because our church was large enough. When church officials collected the offering, my friends and I would sneak out of church and joyride through the city. To show you how young and stupid we were, we would sneak out and visit other churches to see the girls there. We would return to our church early enough to get the scripture the preacher preached from in case our parents questioned us.

Finally, I enjoyed hanging out with these guys because although they were all amusing, Jay was the funniest because he was notorious for capping (playing the dozens). In fact, Jay could talk so badly about someone that it could be traumatizing because he always would throw low blows, which were "Yo momma" jokes. Now, when I think about it, I even hung around him because I did not want to be on the receiving end of Jay's caps.

One of the things Jay used to do, which we all thought was funny but odd, was "catch the Holy Ghost." For instance, when the energy (spirit) was high and the music was playing in the church, Jay would get the Holy Ghost and start shouting (dancing) like the people slain by the spirit. He would speak in tongues and the whole bit, but when the music died down, he would return to his usual self.

I always found this odd because Jay would get the Holy Ghost and then lose it, but it never made Jay a better person. Then, one day, it happened. Jay and I got into it and capped on each other for five minutes straight. Jay went low and started with his "Yo momma" caps as usual. I managed to hang on and keep capping with Jay for a while because my mother told me not to take it personally when someone talked about her since it was not true, and capping was only done for laughs. But Jay didn't let up, and eventually, he crossed the line and started saying some pretty malicious things about my family that he promised not to share as a friend.

So, I began to distance myself from him and the others after that day. Eventually, I stopped hanging out with them all together. Several years later, I was saddened to learn that Jay had become ill and had died while the other two guys were serving time in prison for committing some very heinous crimes.

The Real Meaning of Ra

I used to wonder why the Holy Ghost never transformed Jay until a better person. When I got older, I learned that the Holy Ghost in

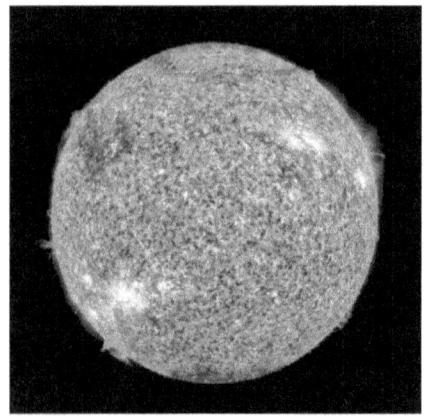

the Kemetic tradition is called Ra. Contrary to popular belief, Ra or Rau is not the sun god but was symbolized by the Sun to illustrate that the Ra(u), or the Holy Ghost, is an unadulterated power.

To understand why Rau was represented as the Sun, we must realize that life on Earth is maintained and sustained because of the power of the Sun. If the

Sun did not exist, for one, vegetation would disappear, and life on the planet would end. So, the Kemetic sages felt and thought we need the physical Sun to live. We also need the spiritual Sun to live because the Rau or Kemetic Holy Ghost is the Life Force, or the Spirit, and the Power of God that gives us the power, knowledge, and information on how to accomplish our goals.

A more contemporary symbol for the Rau would be a bonfire or campfire.

Imagine a bonfire or campfire and how hot it gets. The closer you get to the bonfire or campfire, the more the heat intensifies.

Meanwhile, the farther away you are from the bonfire, the less the heat intensifies or gets colder.

Suppose we think about how the Rau permeates every aspect of life regardless of our wisdom and intelligence. Put it bluntly, the Rau animates the lowest lifeform to the highest. In other words, Rau permeates every aspect of our life. The Rau is in our air, food, water, ground, etc. because it is the Kemetic Chi. Since the Rau is in the air, we breathe. Since air does not discriminate between the young and old, the ugly and the pretty, the in-shaped and out-of-shaped, the healthy and unhealthy, the dumb from the wise, the racist and the tolerant, etc., this is proof that we all have access to the Rau and that the Divine does not discriminate, play favorites or have a chosen person or a chosen group of people.

Thinking about the bonfire analogy mentioned above, you would not have a child go to the bonfire because they would burn themselves and others. We don't let children go to the bonfire or play around the fire because the child does not have the knowledge, wisdom, understanding, skillset, etc., of how to approach the fire. It is common sense. A child around a fire would not only burn themselves but could catch other things on fire, and it would be disastrous.

Instead, you would allow more experienced individuals to approach the bonfire. You would let a more experienced individual stoke or poke the fire and fuel it to get it to burn higher.

An even more experienced individual, you would allow them to use the bonfire to safely create a means to hang a coffee or teapot to make beverages. An even more experienced individual could cook a one-pot meal using the fire. An individual with superior skills could use that fire to boil a pot of food, bake bread, make coffee/tea, and take one of the embers from the fireplace and use it to warm up another part of the house and defend themselves. As you can see, the more knowledge, wisdom, experience, etc., that the individual has, the more they could use the fire safely to improve their life and the lives of others.

Who Are the Ancestral Spirits that Walk With Us?

In Afro-Kemetic spirituality, we could say, using the fireplace analogy, that a **child of fire** or a **"child of the Rau"** is what the Kemetic people called Set. From this analogy, I hope you can see that Set (Set-an or Satan) is not the epitome of evil but does not know how to work the Rau without harming themselves and others. The ancestral spirits associated with Set are called aapepu, which are symbolized as noxious snakes and poisonous worms because they are chaotic, confused, misguided, and wayward ancestral spirits. In the Kongo, these spirits are called bankuyu and are believed to be transformed into bisialala or lizards.

The individual who is more experienced or has developed the skill set to work with the fire or the Rau could be rightfully called a **man and woman of fire** or "**Man and Woman of the Rau**," which

the Kemetic people called Osar (Osiris). Again, from this analogy, I hope that you see that this is not about good versus evil but knowledge, wisdom, and power. Hence, everyone in Kemet strove to be Osar-like because it was the highest honor of respect. When an individual achieved being Osar-like, it indicated that they were a knowledgeable and wise member of society who could improve their life and the lives of others. For this reason, the ancestral spirits associated with Osar are called aakhu because they were revered and honored ancestors and spirit guides, called Kikongo bakulu.

We have both aakhu (bakulu) and aapepu (bankyuyu) who walk with us because both spirits accompany us from birth, while other spirits accumulate throughout life. All these spirits contribute to our spiritual development and help shape our character. This means that Jay could catch the Holy Ghost. Still, it never entirely transformed him because we all have positive and negative forces that surround us constantly. However, the spirits that influence our lives the most are those we give the most time and attention to.

In other words, unlike physical growth, spiritual growth does not occur by default. Spiritual growth, like emotional maturity, occurs only when we consciously choose to grow spiritually. When we consciously choose to grow spiritually, we attract the aakhu and their blessings of wisdom, power, etc. However, if we do not consciously decide to grow spiritually, we will not grow spiritually and will attract the aapepu.

Jay managed to channel his lower ancestral spirits or the aapepu. If we had been adequately educated about these lower spirits, we could have encouraged Jay not to listen and follow the advice of these spirits. We could have also been spiritually cleansed to drive these spirits away from us. Still, none of this happened because we didn't know any better. Instead, the Holy Ghost did not transform Jay because he did not choose to be. As a result, the spirits he attracted to himself influenced him and those around him for the worst. This is important to note because there are a lot of people who believe that spirits can compel them to do something. People always say that the devil (such as money, food, some individual, etc.) made them do something. If the devil (money, food, etc.) did not physically make you do it, it did not compel you to do anything. The truth is that spirits will only encourage you to do what is in your heart (thought), and the type of spirits you attract to you will be reflected in your Ka (personality).

For example, money doesn't make you evil. Money only enhances what you already are. If you are a jerk, when you come into a windfall of money, money will only make you a bigger jerk. Does it make sense why the Rau is symbolized as a fire now?

Therefore, if you are always having a negative experience, it may be because you have a negative heart and have attracted negative spirits to you. Suppose you are happy and relatively content with life. In that case, it may be because you have a positive or balanced heart and have attracted positive spirits.

How do we attract positive spirits to us? It is through honoring the Ancestors.

CHAPTER 5:
How to Build an Altar for Your Aakhu (Ancestors & Spirit Guides)

The one thing that needs to be understood about ancestors and spirit guides is that they will never interfere with your free will, a crucial difference between your aakhu (ancestors and spirit guides) and aapepu (chaotic, confused, and misguided low ancestors). If you want help, it's up to you to ask for their help because the aakhu will not voluntarily offer you any advice or guidance. If you wish their advice or guidance, you have to ask for it, and the best way to do this is through venerating your ancestors.

Ancestor veneration is one of the oldest (if not the oldest) spiritual traditions in the world. People worldwide have performed it because what happens after death has always been a mystery to humanity. As a result, every culture that has walked the planet has created its theories about this phenomenon because all normal people wish and hope that they will rest in peace in the afterlife.

The Kemetic people were no exception. Everything from the elaborate rituals performed on the bodies of the deceased noble class to the folk practices conducted by the Kemetic laypeople are all rooted in their desire to rest in peace in the afterlife. This is why ancestor veneration was a highly regarded practice in the Kemetic tradition. It is important to remember that the reason for honoring the ancestors and venerating the spirit guides from a Kemetic practitioner perspective is because the ancestors and spirit guides who are familiar with the physical realm and reside in the spiritual realm can offer insight into how to live in the physical realm.

Just like there are many ways to honor the ancestors, there are many ways to build an ancestor altar. I like to honor my ancestors on a unique ancestral altar commonly called a bóveda espiritual (spiritual tomb) or bóveda (for short) in Spanish. This particular altar comes from the Afro-Caribbean and Latin American Spiritist traditions inspired by the mid-19th century French philosopher Hippolyte Léon Denizard Rivail, better known by his pen name Allan Kardec. For the record, I didn't believe in spirits because I grew up in an Apostolic Pentecostal household. We were only taught to think in two types of spirits: the spirits of God and the spirits of the devil. The spirits of God were called the Holy Ghost. In contrast, the spirits of the devil were the spirits of envy, backsliding, gossiping, anger, illness, etc., which made me fear all spirits.

Years later, when I began learning about Spiritism through my mentor Papa, I only subscribed to the practice because I had learned that Rivail proved that spirits existed and that there were more benevolent spirits than malevolent ones. Rivail, a French educator with a Bachelor of Arts in science and a doctorate in medicine, began investigating Spiritualism to determine if there was any scientific reasoning behind the phenomenon. Rivail accomplished this by performing double-blind experiments where he asked anonymous mediums a series of questions to see if there were any discrepancies in their responses. After finding each medium, I anonymously gave the same response to over 1,000 or more questions. He concluded that there was a host of spirits. Some spirits were malicious, but many were intelligent and wise and wanted to help humanity spiritually evolve. He published his research in *The Spiritist Book*, which codified the spiritualist practice and introduced the philosophy known today as Spiritism. Spiritism was chosen instead of Spiritualism to distinguish between the two. Spiritism is a philosophy that believes in elevating the soul via reincarnation by relying heavily on Christian ethics and morals, while Spiritualism does not.

In the late 19th and early 20th centuries, Spiritism spread like wildfire through the Western world and significantly influenced Caribbean and Latin-American spirituality. However, Spiritism was short-lived and eclipsed in North America by the Holiness Movement and, later, the Pentecostal Movement. Yet both Movements (especially the Pentecostal Movement) were heavily influenced by Spiritist principles. I learned about Spiritism, specifically Afro-Caribbean and Latin American Spiritism, from my mentor, Papa, who taught me how to honor my ancestors and spirit guides using the bóveda. But my bóveda grew and changed over the years to reflect my Kemetic beliefs. For instance, the term for ancestors in the Kemetic language is aakhu, which translates to "stars," thus indicating that the ancestors are supposed to be our guides like stars act as guides in the night. This understanding helped me see that we have different types of ancestors besides our biological ones, such as cultural ancestors, historical ancestors, and other ancestral spirits willing to assist us. In other words, my bóveda morphed into a het aakhu (ancestor and spirit guide house), and it helped me realize that we are not alone. To communicate with our ancestors and spirit guides, we need to follow two rules, which are:

1. Keep the altar tidy, which means clean your altar at least once a week. Don't allow clutter around it. For this reason, I do not like to place fresh flowers on my altar because I don't want the petals falling all over the place, but that's my preference.
2. Never place photos or images of the living on the altar. Ideally, your ancestor altar should be built in the western part of your dwelling or facing the west because the west

is the direction of the setting sun and the direction of the ancestors. However, this is not necessary or a requirement; it is part of the tradition. Before erecting the altar, you need to get the following items and spiritually cleanse the space where you will erect the altar.

Ideally, your ancestor altar should be built in the western part of your dwelling or facing the west because the west is the direction of the setting sun and the direction of the ancestors. However, this is not necessary or a requirement; it is part of the tradition. Before erecting the altar, you need to get the following items and spiritually cleanse the space where you will erect the altar.

Spiritually Cleaning Ingredients

- Tap Water
- Florida Water
- Two caps of Ammonia

Other ingredients can be added or substituted from this list, but most people should be able to get these items. What you will do is mix these ingredients in a bucket. Next, with your right hand (your giving hand), say a prayer over the liquid mixture, asking that it remove all negative energies so that constructive and positive spirit communication between your ancestors and spirit guides will occur. Suppose you need help with saying a prayer in your own words. In that case, you can pray Psalms 23rd, which is used as an all-purpose prayer within the African American community. Next, wash down the walls (especially the corners) and the floor where the altar will be built. Once the area has been cleaned, you should feel calm if you do not wash the area down again.

Building an Ancestor Altar

To erect the altar, cover a clean, flat surface (box, shelf, table, etc., preferably made of wood and not plastic) with a white tablecloth. I like to spray some cologne or perfumes like Florida Water on the tablecloth to keep the space smelling fresh. I do this before placing the glasses on the altar.

On top of the altar, place a white candle, fresh flowers, and your favorite incense. You can now put 1, 3, 7, or 9 glasses filled with cool tap water on the altar. I like to use nine glasses (8 glasses with one more oversized glass), which I will explain below. Next, surround the glasses with photos of your deceased family members, but if you had issues with any of the dead relatives, such as them having a criminal past, being abusive, suffering from an addiction, etc. Then, do not place their photo on the altar. Finally, additional items belonging to your ancestors or that will honor and help you remember them, such as crucifixes, statues, dolls, or any of their personal belongings, etc., are also placed on the altar.

It is up to you what items are placed on your altar because the altar goes as you feel. As I said, there is no right or wrong way to build the altar if you follow the abovementioned rules. If something does not feel right on your altar, you can change it because it is your altar, and no one (living or spirit) can tell you what to do with it. If you feel like adding something, do so, but if you want to remove something, take it off because you are the ultimate authority.

As I mentioned, my ancestor altar evolved to reflect my Kemetic beliefs partly because my relationship with my ancestors and spirit guides grew. So, when I first began honoring my ancestors, I started with one clear glass bowl and placed a photo of historical aakhu like Malcolm X and Martin L. King Jr. Then, one day, I took the historical aakhu photos off and began to put my deceased biological aakhu on the altar. Over time, I added statues and figurines to represent my cultural aakhu, which symbolizes my great, great, great grandparents and then Indigenous Americans who walk with me. However, I understand how some people can have spirit guides, like nuns, gypsies, sailors, nannies, etc. I didn't find this to be the case because my family lineage lived in Protestant North America.

My ability to identify the aakhu who walked with me resulted from sitting down, meditating, and talking with my Spirits. The more I spent time with my aakhu, the easier it became for me to recognize the spirits who walked with me. In time, some of these spirits began requesting that I place certain items on my ancestral altar to represent them.

Today, my ancestor's altar comprises nine glasses of cool water with photos, figurines, and various items. For instance, my het aakhu has seashells along the edge to form a protective border and to symbolize the Nyun or Kalunga line. The left side of my ancestor altar is dedicated primarily to my male ancestors because the left side corresponds to the Eye of Ra, which is associated with Shu, heat, aggressiveness (sometimes reckless), defensiveness, light, the sun, expansive, growth, movement, etc. At the same time, the right side corresponds to the Eye of Hru (Horus), which is associated with Tefnut, the cool, receptive, dark, the moon, the oceans, contractive, contemplation, intuitiveness, softness, stillness, quiet, etc. Thus, together, they symbolize the opposite yet interconnected and mutually perpetuating forces needed to maintain Maa in my life. In other words, it is a reminder to be holistic. So, on the left-hand side, I have a statue of an elderly Black Man to symbolize my great-great grandfathers and a statue of a Native American spirit guide who assisted my family in escaping slavery. On the right-hand side is an elderly Black Woman statue symbolizing my great-grandmothers. I also have a statue of a female Native American spirit guide who taught some of my family the food and herbs needed to survive in this new land. I also have a small bible because my grandfather enjoyed reading it every morning.

Because of the first rule, I used to have a plant I would place on the ancestor altar, but I stopped doing so because I didn't like it if I poured too much water into the plant. It would spill over and soil my white cloth. I used to put flowers on the altar, but I did not like the petals falling over the altar and inside the glasses of water. So, I occasionally put flowers on my altar, but usually, I avoid it. So, as you can see, you are free to place or take away any item on the altar as you see fit and how it makes you feel. If the item helps you feel relaxed, go for it because it is up to you.

Also, I use nine glasses on my ancestor altar because the number nine is associated with mystery and completion, and the number ten symbolizes the beginning of a new cycle. For instance, it takes nine months for people to be born into the physical realm, and the tenth month begins the new cycle in the physical realm. Therefore, the nine glasses symbolize those who transitioned into the spirit realm. I use nine glasses also because they correspond to the nine netcharu, which, based upon my research and experience, are not gods and goddesses but, as I mentioned in the previous chapter, are aspects, attributes, and principles of Netchar that have been personified. So, the nine glasses symbolize the nine netcharu and the host of ancestral spirits or aakhu working harmoniously as tribal clans for a common cause, like the netcharu, according to some interpretations of the legend, had done to build and maintain the Kingdom of Osar (Osiris).

The nine glasses reflect my diverse ancestry, which is composed of numerous ethnicities due to colonization and slavery. Through the nine glasses, I pay homage and honor my Bantu, Yoruba, Akan, Native American, and other cultures that made me. The largest glass of the nine glasses celebrates the leading ancestral spirit who guides me.

Ancestor Offerings

Once all the items are on the ancestor altar, you are ready to make offerings to your ancestors. Since the ancestors do not have a physical body, they cannot consume the food and drink you offer them. However, they can absorb the essence of the offerings made to them. Here is a list of items that you can offer to your ancestors:

- Cooked food – I usually offer a plate of food to my ancestors once a month.
- Liquor – I offer my ancestors a small shot of liquor. However, whiskey and vodka are the most common liquors that were drunk. I sense that my ancestors prefer white rum. A little shot glass of liquor is needed. You don't want them to get drunk.
- Beer – You can offer beer. I do not offer beer to my ancestors because every time I place it on my altar, a mold grows on it, which violates the first rule.
- Coffee – Offering your ancestors strong black coffee is good because it makes them alert. I typically get good results whenever I offer it without sugar.

- Candies and Gum – Some of our ancestors had a sweet tooth, so I offer a few candies. My grandmother loved those nasty mints and chewing gum, so I offer these items instead.
- Bread & Pastries – I used to offer these, but again, I stopped because of the clean-up. Also, I don't like my pets trying to eat food off the altar.
- Cigars and Tobacco Products – I have ancestors who liked to smoke cigars, cigarettes, and chewing tobacco. These are all offerings that I offer my ancestors.

To Honor Your Aakhu - Your Ancestors and Spirit Guides

Since the ancestor altar acts as a portal or doorway between the two realms (spiritual and physical):

1. Knocking thrice on the altar or on the floor in front of it is customary. Although knocking is a ceremonial gesture meant to put you in a contemplative mood, instead of knocking, some people prefer to use a small bell that they can ring, which is like a doorbell or a shopkeeper's bell. In addition, I burn incense, herbs, or roots such as palo santo, sage, or even tobacco and say a prayer to the spirits of Npu, who sit at all crossroads, asking permission to meet with my aakhu. It is beneficial to state your intention, so you stay focused. Metaphorically speaking, entering the spirit realm without an intention is like walking into a darkroom with a blindfold and no clear destination.
2. Next, safely light a white candle, which could be glass-encased, a white taper candle, tealight, etc., and allow it to burn away from combustible items.

You can say any prayer that you like or are comfortable with. I was taught to first pray from the heart, which is done by simply expressing gratitude to the Divine and the ancestors for all your blessings and things you are grateful for. Afterward, you ask that your ancestors protect you and your family and that they guide you in your decision-making. In addition, you can request that your ancestors act as guards and warn you of impending danger.

The second way I was taught to pray was to use Allan Kardec's *Collection of Selected Prayers* because there were prayers for everything in this little book. I did not like using these prayers because although Kardec was a Spiritist, he aligned Spiritism with Christian ethics and principles. So, a lot of the prayers refer to men and women as sinned creatures. Instead of appealing to the Divine and spirits for help, many prayers sound like they are begging for salvation. Instead, I chose to use the Psalms because, for one, my ancestors were familiar with them, and second, the Psalms are empowering when read metaphysically. Again, Psalms 23rd can be used to honor the ancestors.

3. Once the candles extinguish themselves, thank your ancestors. The ritual is complete.

CHAPTER 6:
What are the Netcharu (Guardian Spirits) and How Do You Build an Altar for Them?

Remember, the nine glasses symbolize the nine spiritual clans and are used to honor all your aakhu; however, if you choose to go beyond this level because you feel a particular connection to one of the netcharu. Making a specific altar for the netchar, called a het netchar or guardian spirit house, would be helpful.

Before building a het netchar, it is essential to understand that although archeologists and historians claim that the netcharu are gods and goddesses. I have yet to experience this because I am not trying to prove that the Kemetic people worshipped idols. I am simply trying to improve my life. This is why I cannot stress enough how important it is to see the netcharu as a personification of the various aspects of your collective unconscious. Once it is accepted that these divinities represent the dimensions within the universe that are mirrored within your mind, you will awaken to the beauty and transformative power within this tradition.

Once I began to believe that the netcharu were personified dimensions within my mind, I began to see the netcharu as a deified ancestral spirit or archetype that symbolizes the elemental forces that exist in nature, spiritual vibrations, or forces of energy. When individuals physically die, they transition and gravitate to the energy or archetype that resonates with them the most in life. So we have it that if an individual was a soldier in life, in death, that individual may gravitate to the warrior netcharu Hru Aakhuti and serve as a guardian spirit who protects you from psychic attack or protects you by helping you to filter unwise advice that may lead you astray. This metaphysically is allegorized by stating that the netcharu do not incarnate because they are too highly evolved. Instead, they send the aakhu as their emissaries, which is how the netcharu can answer petitions worldwide. The aakhu may but most likely are not spirits, you know, but they can and will assist you in achieving your goal under the guidance of the netchar.

There are ten netcharu, and the spirits that walk with them or the spiritual clans, and they are as follows:

Osar

Osar (Asar, Osiris) is the firstborn and eldest of the netcharu. Osar

is regarded as the founder of the Kemetic civilization. Osar is associated with mountains, the sky, and the Underworld (Amenta, Duat, the underground).

In Kemetic lore, Osar came to power when his people were warring among themselves. Some sources say he spoke with Djahuti, desiring to end the senseless wars and spread peace throughout the land. The two devised a plan that led Osar to teach the people about Maa, which brought peace and prosperity to the land and eventually the kingdom (and world). But, due to his popularity, Osar was murdered by his youngest brother, Set, and his throne was usurped. Thankfully, Osar's sister-wife Oset magically conceived an heir for Osar, named Hru, who would grow up to challenge Set and reclaim the throne. was more. Since Set was more knowledgeable and experienced in warfare than the young Hru, Set would always defeat the young prince in battle

until Djahuti revealed to Hru Set's weakness, allowing Hru to defeat Set in battle. Because Set ruled the kingdom for so long, the courts, out of fear, refused to declare Hru, the victor. Then, from beyond the grave, Osar intervened on behalf of Hru and told the court official to follow the Maa and rule out on the premise of what is Right and not out of Might, which is how he will judge them in the Underworld. Hru was declared the kingdom's ruler, while Osar became the ultimate judge and Lord of the Underworld.

Hence, Osar is the ultimate judge of the Underworld. Since the Kemetic religion is historically the oldest spiritual system in the world, Jesus of Nazareth, Our Lady of Mercy, and others are seen as Osar's avatars. In other words, these are forms that the spirits of Osar will choose to speak through. These spirits of Osar are identified by the color white and Osar's animal totems like the dove and elephant.

Consequently, the spirits of Osar are spirits like Osar who are committed to spreading peace, prosperity, and unity. Generally, these spirits are very patient, understanding, and tolerant. Still, they are stern because, as spirits, they know our souls and can see our potential. The spirits of Osar offer us unconditional love, knowledge, and wisdom when it is most needed. They are high vibrational spirits that will never leave our side, so most call spirits of Osar our guardian angels. The largest goblet on the ancestor altar is dedicated to the spirits of Osar because they are like the office manager to all your spirits, organizing and managing them so that nothing is too chaotic all at once.

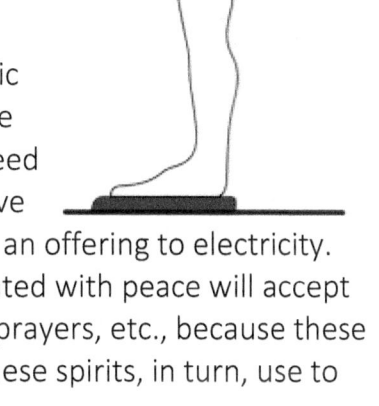

In my experience of practicing Kemetic spirituality, I have found that since the netcharu are energies, they do not need offerings. For instance, you cannot give peace an offering, which is like giving an offering to electricity. However, the ancestral spirits associated with peace will accept the offerings of light (candles), food, prayers, etc., because these offerings elevate their souls, which these spirits, in turn, use to assist us, the living.

Therefore, the spirits of Osar will accept any white offering, such as coconut meat, coconut milk, white eggs, white rice, white potatoes, white yams, cassava (yuca), etc. However, the spirits of Osar are primarily fond of personal commitment or sacrifice as an offering, such as the sacrifice or promise to give up vices like alcohol, smoking, overeating, etc.

Djahuti

In Kemetic lore, Djahuti (Djehuty, Thoth) was responsible for  recording divine events (Akashic records), maintaining the cosmic order, and in the judgment of souls in the afterlife, he was responsible for recording the results of the weighing of the heart against the feather of Ma'at. All the legends of Djahuti reference him as the wisest of the netcharu and, therefore, the creator of writing, mathematics, and magick.

Although the cyclic phases of the Moon are associated with Djahuti, reflecting the waxing and waning of knowledge and wisdom, Djahuti is related to the planet Jupiter (Major) for its abundance. Some sources state that Djahuti is Ma'at's husband, but this is metaphorical language to explain how wisdom, balance, and order are complimentary and interdependent. The number 8 is sacred to Djahuti; his colors are blue and white. Djahuti's totem animals are cranes, storks, ibis, owls, baboons, and turtles. Djahuti is syncretized with the biblical King Solomon. Sacred objects are quills, divination, and scrying tools. Djahuti is the patron of shamans, diviners, metaphysicians, alchemists, and mathematicians.

Since Djahuti was the wisest of the netcharu, Kemetic lore indicates that he was the only netchar that Set truly feared because Djahuti could easily see through Set's devious plans, find his weakness, and determine Set's downfall.

The spirits of Djahuti are teaching guides that help us learn lessons to achieve our destiny. They are wise, creative, and practical spirits that typically bring us good or bad experiences that force us to reassess our situation and make the necessary changes to our path. When these spirits are asked for assistance or guidance, they typically appear in our dreams when we meditate or may leave subtle signs for us to pick up on. Most people are afraid of their spirits of Djahuti because, egotistically, they fear change, which is allegorized in the *Story of Osar*, as Set being afraid of Djahuti.

It should be noted that the spirits of Djahuti, because of their association with the Moon, also oversee synchronicity. Therefore, whenever you see repeating numbers or patterns, it is a sign from these spirits either informing you that you are on the right course or need to be. The spirits of Djahuti also have access to our

Akashic Records (past, present, and future), which is why they are to change fate with their wisdom.

The spirits of Djahuti will accept most offerings given to the spirits of Osar but are higher spirits like the spirits of Osar. The spirits of Djahuti are primarily fond of personal commitment or sacrifice as an offering or form of payment. When these spirits give you insight that improves your life, they want you to spread the word about how Set fears Djahuti.

Sokar-Ptah

The netchar Sokar Ptah is a combination of the Sokar, the falcon-headed netchar associated with death and the afterlife, combined with the bald mummified man, associated with building and craftsmanship, to symbolize the power of renewal, rebirth, and resurrection. In other words, Sokar Ptah represents determination, perseverance, and resiliency found in those who choose to beat the odds, like patients who defeated cancer.

Unlike the warrior netchar Hru Aakhuti, who works hard and fast, Sokar is in it for the long haul. For this reason, the Sokar Ptah is associated with healing –mainly incurable and infectious illnesses. The longsuffering aspect of the disease is symbolized as Sokar, while the recovery from it is represented as Ptah. Sokar Ptah is associated with the planet Saturn. The numbers 13 and 17 are sacred to Sokar. Sokar Ptah is syncretized with the biblical Job, the Lazarus of the Jesus parable, and Saint Alex or San Alejo.

Sokar-Ptah is the patron of the cemetery and mortuary workers, and those who support the infrastructure like miners, repair personnel (e.g., telephone, cable, plumbers, and all who work underground to ensure essential services are maintained). Sokar

Ptah's colors are black, white, brown, or purple. Totem animals are owls, vultures, old birds of prey, and tortoises.

The spirits of Sokar-Ptah are master planners and great healers who want to ensure that our desires, goals, and wishes manifest at the right time. These spirits are humble and slow-acting, but their assistance and guidance are thorough and long-lasting. The spirits of Sokar-Ptah help us plan and follow plans.

The spirits of Sokar Ptah are fond of rum, dark ales, cigars, dry white wines, dates, raisins, sesame seeds, grains, and legumes. However, like the spirits of Osar and Djahuti, Sokar Ptah spirits desire the most that you testify about the greatness of the Divine Spirit to be humble, patient, persevering, determined, and unwavering.

Maat (Ma'at)

The personification of the principle of Maa is Ma'at, who is said to be the sister-wife of Djahuti. Some other sources say that Ma'at is the sister-wife of Hru Aakhuti, who curtails the warrior netchar from going too far in dispensing justice.

Although Ma'at is the personification of balance, law, righteousness, and truth, she is the guardian spirit of love and mercy. She encourages us to place the needs of others above our own. Consequently, Ma'at is the patron of judges, attorneys, economists, and police officers. Ma'at's colors are light blue, sky blue, and yellow. The numbers 2 and 4 are sacred to Ma'at, and the planet Jupiter (minor) is associated with her.

Ma'at energy can be found at sacred hills and mounds, forests on the edge of town, and courthouses. Ma'at's totem animals are ostriches, and objects sacred to her are handcuffs, cages, ostrich feathers, pistols, earth from sacred mounds, earth from banks, and earth from courthouses. Ma'at is syncretized with John the Baptist, who is recognized as the last protector of the Old Testament.

The spirits of Ma'at are merciful and protective spirits that offer physical and psychic protection by either including or excluding specific energies or spirits from entering our realm of influence. The spirits of Maat's close association with Djahuti give them access to the Akashic Records, thus allowing them to see the past, present, and future. Therefore, the spirits of Maat are like bouncers (or security) at a nightclub that only allows VIP members to enter. If you have ever had a hunch to not do something because it would create an imbalance, resulting in more problems than solutions, this was due to the spirits of Ma'at. The spirits of Ma'at usually work alongside the spirits of Hru Aakhuti and offer a different type of protection.

 The spirits of Ma'at are fond of pears and apples, nuts, corn, rum, and water. They help people see the various existing cycles to establish and maintain balance and righteousness.

Hru Aakhuti

Hru Aakhuti (Hor-em-akhet -Hru on the Horizon, Horakhti,  Harakhty) is known by many names such as Hru-Ur (Hru the Elder), Hru-Behdeti (Hru of Behdet or the winged sun disc of Edfu), and Anhur. He is the second eldest son of Nut and Geb, the brother of Osar, Oset, Set and, Nebthet, and uncle of Hru, the son of Osar and Oset.

The netchar of war is not Hru Aakhuti, the author of confusion; Set is the Lord of War. Hru Aakhuti does not start the war but works hard to end it because he is the chief warrior netchar. Hru Aakhuti is martial energy associated with the planet Mars. He protects one from enemies, helps one find employment, aids in hunting, and assists in any fast, aggressive, and dangerous endeavor. Hru Aakhuti is the patron of construction workers, metal workers, surgeons, fishermen, dock workers, professional athletes, entrepreneurs like in the film The Founder, and high-yield stockbrokers.

Hru Aakhuti's colors are blood red and purple. He can be found on the battlefield, in workplaces, out in the fields, deep in the forests, on construction sites, on foundries, walking alongside railroad crossings, working on docks, and next to Npu, usually around the front door.

The spirits of Hru Aakhuti are protective spirits that protect us mentally, physically, and spiritually. These spirits protect us in various ways, such as helping us filter out bad advice and people. They sound our inner defenses when 'something is not right.' Because Hru Aakhuti works with Maat, the spirits of Hru Aakhuti also assist us in protecting us from future calamity by building up our defenses (physically, mentally, spiritually, etc.).

The spirits of Hru Aakhuti are fond of roasted root vegetables, corn, chili, jerky, wild game meat, nuts, kidney beans, black beans, whisky, and all foods favored by rugged individuals like cowboys, hunters, soldiers, and survivalists. Naturally, Hru Aakhuti being a warrior means that the spirits of Hru Aakhuti are fond of collecting weapons.

Hru (Horus)

The term "hru" has different meanings in the Kemetic language, like "day." Consequently, there are various types of Hru (Horus). The Hru we speak of is the child of Osar and Oset, the heir to the throne of Osar, who is the true lord of justice, power, and victory over enemies. Hru is the epitome of manliness, power, and sensuality. For this reason, Hru energy is symbolized as a lightning bolt. Hru is associated with the Sun and is called upon whenever someone feels disrespected  cries for justice or feels like they have been abused or taken advantage of. Hru is all about honor, being just, and fair. Hru's colors are red, white, and gold. The number 6 is sacred to Hru. Hru's totem animals are hawks (falcons), rams, bulls, stallions, roosters, and lions. Hru is syncretized with the biblical King David, Saint Gerome, Santa Barbara, and Zeus the Lightning Thrower. Hru can be found on the top of trees, all high places, the fireplace, the business desk, and anywhere to get a bird's eye view.

Hru can be found wherever there is authoritative power. Hru is the patron of rulers, presidents, CEOs, managers, supervisors, and charismatic people. Many people think Hru is about being forceful and physically dominating others, but this is untrue.

Most Hru-influenced people are like lions, and people are enamored of them because of their appearance, intelligence, humor, etc. One of Hru's talents that many people miss is his oratory skills, which he learned from his stepbrother Npu as a child. This is why Hru is also the patron of preachers, salespeople, strategists, and people who find a way to get what they want by manipulating others.

Hence, there is a constructive use of power as well as destructive uses of power, such as a blinded Hru, which symbolizes being corrupted by Set and being a tyrant and cruel dictator like Hitler. Good Hrus don't sit on the sidelines dictating what to do; they get on the battlefield and do the work as well. Think about how a good manager is right alongside everyone else because they understand the meaning of teamwork.

Therefore, the spirits of Hru help people, such as managers, presidents, husbands (or single parents), etc., to understand the delicate use of power. In other words, they are all about helping people become better leaders. They remind us that true leaders are courageous and self-disciplined. True leaders know when to lead and follow and don't consider it a blow to their ego. However, leaders are charismatic, well-dressed, intelligent, articulate, etc.

Spirits of Hru reminds us that good leaders are beloved by their people because they are courageous, strong-willed, honorable, passionate, apologetic, and willing to do what is proper and expected, whatever the cost. The spirits of Hru are fond of red apples, plantains, okra, bananas, almonds, corn, peppers, spicy foods, occasionally cigars and tobacco (according to some), red wine, ales, stouts, and liquors. Spirits of Hru are fond of scepters, crowns, axes, hammers, wood staffs, swords, and sledgehammers. They are good at reminding us that a lion doesn't have to prove it is a lion to be respected as a lion.

Nebthet

Fertility, fresh flowing water, such as streams and waterfalls, are  personified as Nebthet (**Nephthys**), who is associated with art, beauty, diplomacy, fertility, intimacy, marriage, sex, relationships, and money (riches or quick money). Nebthet loves fresh, shiny, and glimmer things, which is why she can be found throughout the entertainment industry. She is the patroness of actors/actresses, filmmakers, singers, and TV personalities. She is also the patroness of those in the cosmetic and fashion industry and the patroness of cooks and chefs.

Nebthet is the youngest sister within the Kemetic pantheon who works with other fertility and household spirits like the dwarf netchar Bes. Nebthet is said to be the wife of Set because she symbolizes the ignorance, inexperience, and naivete of young women. For this reason, she is commonly syncretized with Oshun, Lady of Caridad del Cobre, Saint Martha, Aphrodite, Venus, and all energies that use beauty and sweetness to tame a wild heart, and Mary Magdalene. Nebthet's colors are yellow (and gold), green, pink, and coral. Her sacred number is 5.

Her sacred spaces are parks, river shores, botanical gardens, the kitchen, and the main bedroom. Her totem animals are peacocks, cats, female big cats, ducks, pheasants and parrots. She loves jewelry, bells, mirrors, combs, and seashells.

The spirits of Nebthet are creative, joyful, and all-around happy spirits that encourage us to be happy and optimistic all the time. These spirits remind us that happiness should not depend on money, people, etc. because happiness is ethereal. This means that the only thing that can make us happy is us. Therefore, the spirits of Nebthet encourage us to spread joy and do what makes us happy.

The spirits of Nebthet are fond of all the things that Nebthet loves, including honey, spinach, cinnamon, mangoes, strawberries, peaches, pumpkins, oranges, passion fruits, light pastries, seafood, champagne, and dessert wines.

Npu (Enpu, Anubis)

According to some lore, Nebthet could not conceive a child with her husband Set, which is symbolized by the arid desert and hence sterile. Nebthet conceived a child named Npu (Anubis, Enpu) with Osar. Metaphysically speaking, this signifies how Osar is fertile and life-producing, while Set is sterile. Some sources allege that Nebthet did not raise Npu because if Set had learned the truth about Npu, he would have murdered the child out of his jealousy for Osar. Other sources indicate that Nebthet did not raise Npu because she was too young and lacked mothering skills. Whatever the case, Npu was raised by Oset, thus becoming Hru's older brother. Consequently, Npu has his father Osar's temperament, his mother Nebthet's creativeness and immaturity, his stepmother Oset's love and nurturing, and his stepfather Set's

mean streak, thus making Npu a playful, intelligent, and curious netchar, which are character traits commonly found in children.

Red, black, white, and yellow are the colors

associated with Npu. The number 3 and its multiples and variations, such as 9 and 21, are Npu's sacred numbers. Some of the Kemetic paths associated with Npu are the crocodile-masked Sebek and the wolf-masked ApUat (the Opener of the Way), the Catholic saint Infant of Atocha or Nino de Atocha, and the 12-year-old Jesus (numerology 12 is 1+2=3) in the Jerusalem temple who was separated from his parents for three days are all seen as avatars of Npu. Mercury was called Sebek in ancient Kemet and is associated with Npu.

The spirits of Npu are clever, ingenious, funny, and sometimes tricky spirits that will help us to find a solution to almost anything. These spirits have a knack for making the impossible possible. Whenever something seems impossible and suddenly things fall into place, it is because your Npus are on the case. Hence, the reason Npu is called ApUat or the Opener of the Way.

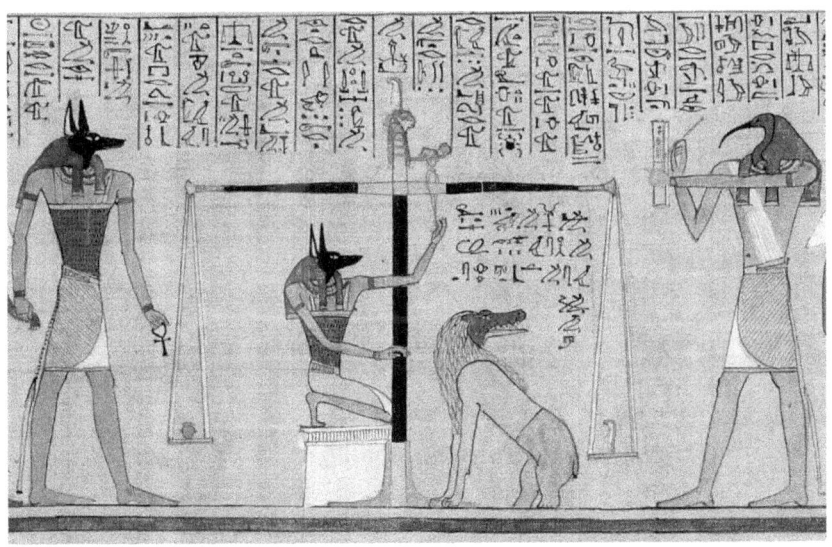

Therefore, the spirits of Npu can be found wherever there are pathways, roads, and doors. Npu spirits are typically playful spirits who like to play games and are very fond of toys, candies, and things all curious kids like and enjoy. The spirits of Npu can appear as children or as older adults.

They are brutally honest, like children who will say whatever comes to their mind with no filter because they have not yet learned what is appropriate and inappropriate. They are great at finding lost things, hence why Npu is found weighing the hearts of the dead against the feather of truth (Maa). Since Npu can find anything, the spirits of Npu are also excellent guides and communicators, but if they feel unappreciated at any time. They will get distracted, wander off, get lost, or lead you astray, thus having you "crossing" your lines so that you become confused.

Oset (Aset, Isis)

The Great Queen Mother of Kemet is named Oset (Aset, Isis), and she is symbolized by a throne because she is the foundation of Kemetic spirituality. In ancient times, Oset was beloved by many because of her undying love for Osar, her strong, motherly, and protective love for Npu and Hru, and her sisterly love for her younger siblings Nebthet and Set. As such, Oset is the personification of motherly love to care for all living beings, which is universally recognized as the seven seas to provide water and food for everyone. Oset was one of the most popular netchar in the Kemetic tradition, with temples found throughout Kemet and Europe because Oset provided and protected those who could not provide and protect themselves.

Oset symbolizes mature and fertile women, whereas Nebthet symbolizes immature and fertile women. Unlike Nebthet, who is dainty, selfish, childish, and unaccountable, Oset is elegant, sophisticated, caring, and responsible. For this reason, Oset can be found everywhere there is a need to administer care, such as in daycares. As such, she is the patroness of mothers, foster care providers, nurses, and other care providers, like caregivers in maternity wards, hospitals, and assisted living facilities.

Oset's colors are blue (sea) and white. Her sacred number is 7, and the Moon is associated with her. Oset's totem animals are fish, shorebirds, cows, sheep, and scorpions. Objects sacred to her are thrones, crescent Moon, fishing nets, anchors, conch shells, sailboats, and seashells. Oset is syncretized with the Yoruba orisha Yemaya, the Catholic saint Our Lady of Miraculous Medals, and the Virgin Mary. Oset is greatly respected for her magical abilities, which she used to conceive the child Hru, the heir of Osar.

The spirits of Oset are excellent spirits that will help you accomplish any task. The task doesn't matter; if you need help, these spirits will help you achieve the goal. For instance, the spirits of Oset assist with infertility issues in women, protection for pregnant women and children, parenting assistance, and child safety. Spirits of Oset are fond of water, beer, watermelons, cantaloupes, molasses, cornmeal, saltwater candy, seafood, and pineapples.

Set (Seth)

Why does the Divine allow evil to exist? The answer can be found in understanding the nature of Set, the youngest brother in the Kemetic lore and the great usurper of Osar's throne. Unlike the Christian Satan, Set is not the epitome of evil, nor is he the chief adversary of the Supreme Being. Adopting the belief that Set is evil contradicts the perfect nature of Netchar. It suggests that Set is not part of the divine plan. For this reason, Set symbolizes everything flawed in humanity. He represents our fears, ignorance, selfishness, arrogance, stupidity, etc. because Set is the personification of our ego.

So, why does the Divine allow Set to exist? It is because Set is our greatest adversary, which means without an adversary or an opponent to challenge us, most people would not strive to be better.

Set does not have any spirit helpers per se, but all negative, chaotic, confused, and misguided ancestral spirits or aapepu fall under his rulership. Since the number 10 signifies the start of a new cycle and the physical realm, it is recognized as Set's sacred number.

Because Set can do bad all by himself, we do not honor or petition Set for assistance because it is like a storm or tempest. Set is unethical and unpredictable, and he does not fight fair. He knows no bounds, so all forms of catastrophe that do not discriminate are authored by Set, such as war, wildfires, floods, landslides, avalanches, tornadoes, hurricanes, earthquakes, etc.

How to Build an Altar for the Netcharu

Here are some brief instructions on building an altar to the netchar and developing a rapport with the netchar.

Since the netcharu are viewed as deified ancestors with a host of spirits beneath them, it is assumed that, like the living, when they are called upon unexpectedly, they may not be home, so they allow lower spirits to assist and act in their place. This is how the netcharu can be in different places simultaneously, so remind yourself of this:

- First, when you build the ancestor altar, clean the space with a good cleaner.
- Second, get an image of the netchar. This can be a figurine, statue, picture, etc.
- Third, get either a ceramic box or pot, such as a planter plate, and dedicate it to the netchar you want to work with by using the colors and the sacred number of the netchar.
- Finally, miniature plaster skulls or skeletons should be purchased to symbolize the spirits of the netchar.

These are the basic items needed to attract the spirits of the netchar to your altar. Building this type of altar requires that you trust your intuition. As your connection with the spirits of the netchar grows, you will get hunches of different items to place on the altar, like herbs, precious stones, crystals, rocks, manmade items, etc. You will be able to identify which netchar the spirit is associated with by the attributes of the items (colors, number, etc.) you are inspired to put on the altar. These items inspired by the netchar's spirits will help you connect with the netchar by stirring your feelings. They will also help you to manifest your desires. You will know that the inspiration is coming from the spirits of the netchar because, along with stirring your feelings, it will feel oddly normal.

For instance, I knew that Npus likes toys and that Npu's colors are primarily red and black. That's why I wasn't surprised one day when I was driving early one morning and came to a four-way stop across from the courthouse. I stopped and exited my car because I thought I had hit something. There, on the side of the road, next to my car, was a red and black toy Jeep. Puzzled, I asked out loud, "How in the hell?" Then, when I looked at the colors, I knew it was my Npus. You never know what the spirits need or do with these things in their realm. So, I thanked my Npus, picked up the toy, and took it home. I purified the toy by spraying it with rum and smoke and gave it to the Npus, who apparently needed some "wheels" (laugh). Today, this toy Jeep has three miniature skeletons, reminding me that the Npus protect me while I am on the road.

CHAPTER 7:
How to Honor & Petition the Netcharu (Guardian Spirits)

Suppose you have erected a het netchar altar, regardless of how big or small your altar is for the spirits of that netchar. These spirits need to be fed weekly to maintain the relationship between you and them. If they are not fed weekly, the relationship between you and them will weaken when you need their assistance. Mustering the spiritual energy to achieve your goals will take a lot of work.

- Offer a small shot glass of water and a white candle. Tell the spirits of the netcharu that you offer them light and water. Then, repeat the small praise phrase in your own words.

To Petition the Netcharu

It is easy to "get lost in the sauce" when working on your Kemetic spirituality because you must remember that the Kemetic tradition is at least 3,000 years old. This means that a lot of metaphysics, interpretations, and syncretism occurred. A significant part of this confusion stems from the fact that most archeologists and historians, blinded by their biases, set out to explain the Kemetic philosophy from the perspective of proving how superstitious the Kemetic people were instead of how pragmatic their philosophy was and how it was necessary for the peacefulness of the Kemetic society. Because of this bias, it is often completely overlooked that the Kemetic tradition had at least five schools of thought, denominations, or sects, including Atenism, like many organized religions today. When this is kept in mind, the secret to working on your Kemetic spirituality is based upon understanding two key concepts:

Since our universe is composed of a known, visible, and logical physical reality and an unknown, invisible, illogical spiritual reality.

1. Magick, prayers, and rituals used for spiritual purposes must be performed with complete confidence, faith, and patience, trusting that the Spirits (Netchar, netcharu, aakhu, etc.) know what is best for you. In other words, there is no logical explanation for why magick, prayer, and rituals work because they are based upon the ethereal, so if you analyze it. It will cease to work, so don't analyze it. Just accept it as one of the mysteries of the Divine. All the spirits are aspects and attributes of the Divine.
2. For instance, instead of saying God is my protector, I pray to God for protection. The protective aspects and attributes of God were called Hru Aakhuti. Instead of saying that God is my provider or El Shaddai, the Kemetic people would say Hru Aakhuti. Instead of saying God is my provider or Elohim, the Kemetic people would say Osar, and so on.

I hope you see that Kemetic spirituality is not a religion but a technology for working your spirit.

Therefore, the simplest way to petition the aakhu and netcharu is to accomplish your goals to the best of your ability. However, when you need help finding the material resources to achieve the desired change, you must leave this physical dimension, reach out to the spiritual dimension, and ask for assistance. Although unnecessary, better and faster results are obtained when you promise to give an offering in return as a symbol of gratitude once the request is answered. To feed your aakhu or netcharu and develop a rapport with them, it is incredibly beneficial to attribute any success related to your petition to the aakhu or netcharu. For instance, if you ask the aakhu or netcharu for help completing a task such as passing an exam. You would first study for the exam as if you already passed the exam. This means something different for each individual but may include analyzing students who have consistently received A's in the subject. Or you are receiving tutoring from someone who has mastered the subject. Your time and commitment are considered a sacrifice for getting what you want. Still, you can ask the aakhu or netcharu if they can help you pass the exam. You will promise to give them an offering. Once you pass your exam, give the spirits an offering such as a candle, candy, or whatever you feel moved to offer. No sacrificing of animals or your pets is required! Remember, these spirits are your ancestral spirits, which means they are concerned about your success and well-being.

Here are a couple of examples:

For Blessings

Take a white taper candle, light the wick end, followed by the base, and place it on top of a penny. Next, ask your spirits to assist you and to give you insight to solve your problem.

For protection

Take your name and write it on a brown such as a brown paper bag that symbolizes the physical body. Write over the name vertically and horizontally to form a cross with the word "Protected." Next, take a spool of red thread and wrap the paper with it while repeating "Protected" aloud or silently to yourself so that the thread has completely covered the paper. Safely light a red candle and place the bundle next to it. Thank Hru Aakhuti for protecting you, and do not ponder on how the spirits of Hru Aakhuti will protect you. Have confidence and faith that you will be protected.

For Personal Transformation

To elevate the character, overcome a negative character feature, improve one's health, or develop a skill, etc. Use a mantra to elevate the character, overcome a negative character feature, improve one's health, or develop a skill. Typically, a mantra is a phrase, a short prayer, or a set of sounds repeated repeatedly to help you focus so that you can achieve a goal. Unlike affirmations, which are directed towards yourself, mantras are repeated multiple times as if the goal has already occurred. For instance, an individual desiring better health would not chant, "I hope I get better," but would repeat instead, "I am healthy," or better yet, "I am healthy and strong."

When a short and direct-to-the-point mantra is repeated as if it has already occurred, it generates an energy that causes the goal to become a physical reality. This should be stated numerous times until you see signs of it manifesting. This was the purpose behind the numerous so-called Kemetic spell books.

CONCLUSION

I hope this book has helped you understand what Kemetic spirituality is and how to start practicing it. Remember, what I have shared on these pages is my understanding of and experience working with the aakhu (ancestors and spirit guides) and the netcharu (guardian spirits). As I mentioned, I continue to practice this spirituality because it allows anyone to merge spirituality and science. Since there is no right or wrong way to practice Kemetic spirituality because it is result-driven, you can tailor my suggestions and advice to address your needs and wants.

You no longer have to guess if God favors you to receive a blessing. You know upfront if you are in alignment with the Divine or not because your Ancestors and spirit guides will tell you. The best thing about this spirituality is that once you trust your intuition. Instead of sitting on the sidelines waiting helplessly for a miracle, you can finally do something about it.

PLEASE REVIEW

Thank you for reading my book and allowing me to share my experience, story, and the methods that I have found that worked for me with you. I hope that this book empowered and improved your life the way it has touched mine.

Please leave a review and let me know what you thought at your favorite retailer. I really appreciate what you have to say.

Also, if you are interested in learning more about the Kamta tradition, you can follow me at:

- thelandofkam.com
- The Land of Kam's Ancestral Way at YouTube
- The Land of Kam on Instagram

Check Out Other Books by the Author:

MAA AANKH Volume I:
Finding God the Afro-American Spiritual Way,
by Honoring the Ancestors and Guardian Spirits

Kamta: A Practical Kemetic Path for Obtaining Power

Maa: A Guide to the Kemetic Way for Personal Transformation

MAA AANKH Volume II:
Discovering the Power of I AM Using the Shamanic Principles of Ancient Egypt for Self-Empowerment and Personal Development

MAA AANKH Volume III:
The Kemetic Shaman Way of Working the Superconscious Mind to Improve Memory, Solve Problems Intuitively and Spiritually Grow Through the Power of the Spirits (Volume 3)

Honoring the Ancestors, the Kemetic Shaman Way:
A Practical Manual for Venerating and Working with the Ancestors from a God Perspective

The Kamta Primer: A Practical Shamanic Guide for Using Kemetic Ritual, Magick and Spirituality for Acquiring Power

En Español: Maa Aankh Volume I:
Encontrando a Dios al Modo Espiritual Afroamericano, Honrando a los Ancestros y a los Espiritus Guardianes

Interested in learning more about Kemetic Spirituality from a shamanic and spiritualist perspective. Visit thelandofkam.com.

Workbooks by the Author:

Obi Abata Divination Journal: For Recording Oracle Results, Consultations and Notes

3 Coin I Ching Divination Journal: For Recording Current and Future Hexagrams

www.ingramcontent.com/pod-product-compliance
Lightning Source LLC
Chambersburg PA
CBHW070303010526
44108CB00039B/1789